A *CopySitter* Author's Guide

Dealing with Constructive Criticism

How to
Handle Constructive Editorial Feedback
and How to Give Feedback to Others

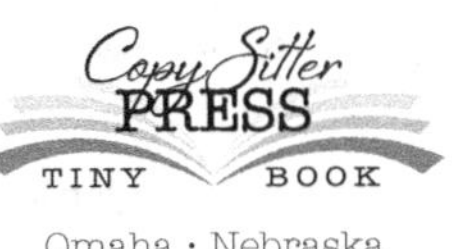

Julie Haase

ISBN-13: 979-8-9986036-0-0 (paperback)

You can find a cavalcade of resources online about how to deal with criticism of all sorts, and most of them start with this idea: Criticism is tough to take.

Duh?

Yes, it's true. Very few of us are so open as to accept criticism without any kind of emotional reaction—whether it's disappointment, anger, defensiveness, bewilderment, or plain old hurt—at one level or another. So how do we take this piece of art we've crafted and turn it over to people whose job it is to pick it apart? Courage and the understanding that this is how we learn, grow, improve, and succeed. Because while it is true that criticism is tough to take, it's equally true—perhaps even more so—that criticism is an essential part of the writer's journey.

So great. That's helpful, right? Do you feel better already? No? Hm, let's see what we can do about that.

Before we can talk about how to deal with it, we need to understand what it is because constructive criticism is very specific and important. One way to understand *constructive* criticism is to view it alongside other types.

Types of Criticism

There are many different types, most of which I'm not going to talk about here because they're simply irrelevant to the topic at hand. However, let's look at a few other types to get some perspective and help better define what is or is not constructive.

Destructive Criticism: This is the worst type of criticism. It's mean and cruel, it's public, and it is intended to do harm.

Negative Criticism: Unlike destructive, negative criticism isn't meant to be harmful, but it isn't all that helpful either. It focuses on the negatives without giving suggestions for how to fix them. Plus, like getting hit over the head repeatedly with a hammer, receiving negative criticism can be headache-inducing.

Positive Criticism: While this criticism might be fun to get, it's not particularly helpful if you're looking for ways to improve. Positive criticism mostly focuses on the good with just a sprinkling of minor issues thrown in.

Constructive Criticism: The gold standard, constructive criticism points out the issues in a respectful way,
includes actionable suggestions, and is not personal.

Constructive Criticism Explained

So what do those three elements of constructive criticism
mentioned above really mean?

Respectful: The criticism is delivered with respect for
the recipient's feelings, abilities, intelligence, etc. It's
given privately, not publicly (but more on this below).

Actionable: The criticism includes specific suggestions
for how to fix the problem.

Not Personal: Constructive criticism addresses the issue, not the person.

In addition, constructive criticism often focuses on
how the behavior affects others (*your coworkers are
having to pick up the slack, which isn't fair to them*). In
writing, those "others"–the recipients of the action, so to
speak–are the readers (*readers may not understand your
meaning here*).

Public vs. Private

Destructive criticism is specifically defined as being public, and constructive criticism is specifically defined as

being private, but in the Internet age, those designations aren't quite fair. To be clear, destructive criticism is public and is *always* public. That's part of what makes it so destructive—the embarrassment and humiliation of being dressed down in front of others.

However, just because criticism is delivered in a public forum does not automatically make it destructive. When it comes to things like online reviews and social media or, closer to our topic here, writing groups, workshops, etc., it's absolutely possible to use constructive criticism effectively. There are certainly those times when it's better to deliver criticism privately, but whether public or private, using constructive criticism is always the way to go.

Examples

To further show the differences between those four types of criticism, let's compare online restaurant reviews.

Destructive

"The food is so vile I was sick for two days! The chef sucks. Don't eat here!"

Yuck! It doesn't say what was actually wrong with the food or how the person was sick (didn't feel well, was actually ill, was just grossed out). It's just mean and angry with the clear intent to harm the restaurant and the chef.

Negative

"The chicken was cold and dry and not very flavorful."

OK. Was there anything good about it? Would they eat there again? Something helpful please!

Positive

"The steak was cooked perfectly, maybe a little less salt, but overall superb."

Nice. A slight hiccup in the middle there, but mostly good, good, good. It won't help the restaurant improve, but pretty lovely for an online review.

Constructive

"The vegetables were a bit bland. Some paprika would really liven them up."

Not that the restaurant is likely to take the suggestion, but who knows? It's respectful, actionable, and it addresses the issue, not the people behind the issue.

Constructive Editorial Criticism

OK, so now that we understand what constructive criticism is in general, let's shift gears and look at a few examples of constructive criticism in the form of editorial feedback and also how that feedback might look if it were decidedly *not* constructive.

Constructive: *It's difficult to keep straight who's doing what here. The inline suggested changes are to fix this problem.*

Not Constructive: *The action is confusing. You haven't explained who's doing what.*

The constructive example is respectful, it's actionable (the inline changes are the actionable suggestions), and it focuses on the issue, not the writer. The non-constructive example is accusatory and does not include a suggestion.

Constructive: *Tamara's motivation isn't clear here. Consider adding an inner thought that explains why she would do this.*

Not Constructive: *Tamara's motivation isn't clear here.*

Again, the constructive example hits all the requirements: respectful, actionable, and not personal. The non-constructive example uses the exact same issue, so it's respectful and not personal, but where is the actionable suggestion?

Constructive: *The description of this maze may be difficult for readers to follow because it's so complex. Consider simplifying the description and using just the elements that readers truly need to know.*

Not Constructive: *You're going to confuse readers with this maze description. It needs to be simplified.*

The constructive example keeps things respectful and not personal by focusing on the reader experience and gives the prerequisite actionable suggestion. The non-constructive is, again, accusatory, it includes a directive instead of a suggestion, and that directive is so vague that's it's not actionable.

As an author, you're likely to find yourself being asked for feedback from other authors, whether in a writing group, from author friends, or in other situations. Regardless of why you're giving the feedback, it's important to ensure that it's constructive.

Here are some tips, by category, for giving good constructive editorial-style criticism.

Be Respectful

Just about every suggestion in this book has an element of respect to it, but here are a few that are specific to achieving this goal.

Remember that suggestions are only *suggestions*.

When you give feedback, you're giving the author your opinions, not cold hard facts. So treat your suggestions as suggestions. When I'm editing, I use phrasing like "please consider" or "perhaps try." This phrasing puts the reins in the author's hands, making it clear that it's up to the author to decide what they want to do. And also …

Don't be bossy.

Choose your words wisely. "Change this" and "You need to" type of wording is just rude. Remember, you're giving suggestions, not directives. Also remember that *the person giving the feedback is **not** in charge*. So when *you're* the one giving the feedback, keep that in mind at all times! And also . . .

Don't be a know-it-all.

I'm in a critiquing writing group, and none of the members in the group are professional editors–except me! And while I have a perspective, knowledge, and experience that the others don't have, I don't know everything. I don't see every problem. And I definitely don't see every solution. Just because I'm the one professional editor in the room doesn't mean I get to act like I know everything. And you shouldn't either. Even if you have knowledge that is specific to what you're critiquing, use your power only for good, not for showing off. Any knowledge you share should be relevant and presented as a teachable (and respectful!) moment, not as an opportunity for you to flaunt how smart you are (not that you would, but please don't).

Make It Actionable

If you've ever gotten editorial or similar feedback, you know that sometimes it's tough to figure out how to fix the problems. That's why actionable suggestions are so important.

Make specific suggestions.

As we've already discussed, actionable suggestions are one of the cornerstones of constructive criticism, so whenever you identify an issue, include a suggestion for how to fix it. For example, if there's a word that's not working for you, suggest another word. Or if a sentence is hard to follow, suggest a rewrite that makes sense to you. Or if a line of dialogue doesn't feel natural, suggest a change. Suggestions help further explain the problem, and while the author might not use your suggestion, it may still help them figure out how *they* want to address the problem.

And be sure those suggestions are specific. Vague suggestions aren't very helpful.

Do your best when you don't know what to do.
Truth be told, you aren't always going to have a suggestion to give. It happens to all of us from time to time. You know there's a problem, but you're just clueless about how to fix it. That's OK! If you don't have a suggestion, explain the issue with as much detail as you can: "Something about this sentence is off to me. I don't know how to fix it. It just reads as awkward to me, like the words are in the wrong order or something. I had to reread it several times, and I'm still not quite sure what it means."

Don't Make It Personal

When giving criticism, make sure you address the issues, not the author. Praise ("You've captured this character beautifully!") can be as personal as you want, but criticism should not be.

Use I statements.

I'm sure you're familiar with this concept. Say things like "I didn't understand this," not "You didn't explain this well." Put the focus on your understanding and experience of the manuscript, not on the author's skills or efforts. You'll give the author a chance to see the issue from a reader's perspective, and you'll avoid putting the author in the hot seat and possibly making them feel attacked or insulted.

Talk about the writing, not the writer.

Don't talk about what the *writer* did or didn't do. Talk about what the *writing* does or doesn't do. For example, say something like "This subplot doesn't seem to connect to the main plot," not "You haven't connected this subplot to the main plot." (Notice how similar this is to using I statements? The point of both is the same—shift the focus away from the author.)

Ask [the right kind of] questions.

Asking questions in a respectful way is a good way to avoid sounding accusatory. Just be sure you avoid "what were you thinking" and passive-aggressive types of questions. Straightforward, content-related questions, though, can present an issue in a thought-provoking, nonconfrontational way: "Why did Clyde hide the money if he thinks Morgan is dead?" not "Why do you have Clyde hide the money when he clearly thinks Morgan is dead?" In other words, ask questions about the writing, not the writer.

Additional Suggestions for Giving Feedback

The following suggestions don't directly relate to constructive criticism, but they're good strategies for delivering effective and useful feedback.

Be specific.

Generalized feedback isn't very helpful. "The plot is hard to follow" doesn't tell the author much. It's OK to start with that, but then you need to get more specific. "The plot is hard to follow because it's not clear why Atreah needs the amulet or how it will save her village." Specificity will help the author know exactly what issue they need to address, making it much easier for them to do so.

Point out what you like too.

When you come across a great description or when a character says something really insightful or when a particular passage makes you laugh really hard, be sure to point it out. Knowing what's working in the writing is just as helpful to an author as knowing what isn't working. Plus it'll make them feel good.

Ask questions.

Hey! Didn't we already talk about this one? Yes, we did! But there's more than one benefit to asking questions. When you ask questions, you force the writer to look at the work from a different angle. This can be eye-opening to the author if they find they don't know the answer to your question. For example, "I don't understand why Lonnie is still outside" might invite a much different response than "Wouldn't Lonnie be inside by now?" The comment gives the author a chance to discount the issue as "your problem," whereas the question forces the author to give an answer–an answer they might not actually have. Boom! You've just saved the day!

Note that it's very helpful to explain why you're asking the question just in case the author *can* answer it. Some authors will assume that if they have the answer, that means there's no issue, so make the issue clear, ensuring that the author can't talk their way out of it.

Explain the benefit the change could have (and the possible consequence if the change isn't made).

In other words, give the author both a reason to make the change and a reason against not making the change: "This would help readers follow your process with greater understanding [benefit of making the change]. Otherwise, they may just get confused and stop reading [consequence of not making the change]." Whenever you can do this, you make it more difficult for the author to argue against making the change, so this is an excellent strategy when you're dealing with a highly important issue.

Ask *yourself* some important questions before giving feedback.

Just because you've identified something you see as an issue doesn't automatically mean it's something that needs to be addressed. Consider the following:

a. **Does the problem need to be fixed?** Ask yourself if you've identified an actual problem or just something that you personally don't like. Also, how big of a deal is this problem? If it's beyond minor, does it really matter? The point here is to identify whether or not you're actually going to be helping the author by pointing it out.

b. **What stage is the manuscript in?** Is this an early draft or a very-nearly-ready-to-be-published draft? As an editor, I really had to retrain my brain for my writing group because we deal mostly with early drafts, and there's no point in fixing people's commas at that point. So consider the stage the manuscript is in before you nitpick at things like punctuation and grammar or other things that are likely to change during revisions. Then again, if it's a late draft, is it helpful to point out that you have an issue with the main character's motivations or is it time to let those big-picture issues go? That really depends on the severity of the issue, so give it some thought first. If it's something that's not likely to impact readers' experience with the book, then you can probably just let it go. Again, if you point it out, will you truly be helping the author?

c. **Can you give actionable suggestions?** As mentioned previously, sometimes we identify issues but we have no idea how to solve them. However, it's also possible that the reason you can't come up with a way to fix a problem is because it's not really a problem at all. Give it some careful thought before you decide how to proceed. If you're confident that the identified issue really does need to be addressed, even without an actionable suggestion, then reread the "Make It Actionable" section and do what you have to do.

d. **Are you grasping for something to criticize or showing off?** When someone asks for a critique, we kind of feel obligated to find things to criticize. But what if you can't find any or you find very little? The last thing you should do is hen-peck the writing to try to find something–*anything*–to criticize. That's not helpful at all. Just give honest feedback, and if there isn't much of it, that's OK. Similarly, don't point out issues as a way of making yourself look smart, and don't overexplain issues to show off how smart you are. Your feedback should always be about the writing, not about you or the author, and it should always have the singular purpose of helping the author improve.

Read twice; criticize once.

Whenever possible, read the manuscript (or segment or story or whatever you're reviewing) at least twice before turning over your feedback. The second readthrough will give you the chance to catch anything you missed, and perhaps more importantly, it will give you a chance to double check your own comments to (1) make sure they all make sense, (2) correct any mistakes you may have made, and (3) confirm that you still agree with yourself. Sometimes what you read later in the manuscript will nullify an issue you identified early in the manuscript, and sometimes you realize that something you thought was an issue the first time through is not an issue at all. These are some of the reasons why professional editors always read a manuscript at least twice.

The bottom line about giving constructive criticism to an author is that you're trying to help them improve the writing and to learn and grow as an author. So ensure that your criticisms are actually *helpful*, and then ensure that they're also respectful, actionable, and focused on the writing, not the writer.

Before we talk about how to handle editorial criticism, let's lay a foundation to ensure we're on the same page (mixed metaphor, anyone?). Some of these suggestions may leave you thinking, "What if it's just a bad edit?" or "What if the suggestions aren't valid?" However . . .

Valid vs. Invalid Criticism

When I talk about editorial criticism, I'm talking about working with editors who are highly experienced, have plenty of expertise in your genre or category (fiction/nonfiction), have knowledge of the industry and market (as applies to your project), and are professionals in the field. I am not talking about amateurs, nonprofessionals, or professionals or otherwise who claim to have knowledge and experience that they don't actually have.

With this in mind, I'm comfortable stating outright that editorial feedback from an experienced and knowledgeable professional with plenty of expertise is going to give you valid feedback every time—whether you agree with that feedback or not. In other words, assuming you've done your due diligence and hired a really good editor, you can assume that their feedback is good. That does not mean, however, that you have to agree with them. But your disagreeing does not invalidate the feedback.

Not to overstate it, but to be clear, *you can disagree with valid feedback*, and it's important to accept that the feedback you've received is, in fact, valid. Otherwise, you

make it way too easy for you to simply discount the feedback you don't like.

"My editor doesn't get me."

Please be wary of this reaction. Some authors will fall
back on this as a defense mechanism when they are very
unhappy about the changes the editor suggests to improve the manuscript. They use this excuse as a way of
invalidating the feedback in order to protect themselves
from having to make changes they don't like.

I've seen this first-hand. I work for an editing and
self-publishing services company, and we offer a variety
of developmental editing services, which authors often
buy in a package of more than one round of service. A few
times since I've been there, authors have finished their
first round and asked to work with a different editor on
the subsequent round, claiming something to the tune
of "The editor didn't understand my purpose" or "The editor didn't understand what I was going for."

In each of these cases, we switched the client to a
different editor who then gave the author essentially the
same feedback the first editor gave.

Now, is it possible for your editor to not get you? Of
course. But is it the norm? Nope. More often than not,
your editor gets you just fine. You just don't like what
they have to say. So if you catch yourself thinking that
your editor doesn't get you, give that some serious con-
sideration before acting on it. Use some of the advice on

the following pages to help you determine what's actually going on.

The Bad Edit

I'm not going to talk about how to recognize a bad edit or what to do if you get one because that's just not what this book is about; however, bad edits do happen and it's a good idea for you to learn about them and how to protect yourself from them.

For the purposes of this book, as I mentioned previously, we're going to assume that the edits you get are good ones, and those are the types of critiques we'll address.

Strategies for Dealing with Editorial Criticism

These strategies are presented in no particular order except that I've put my favorites first.

Accept and Learn

Accepting is all about the thing we just talked about—the validity of the feedback, even if you don't agree with it. It may be difficult to reconcile the fact that editorial suggestions can be valid and *wrong!* at the same time, but consider whether or not "wrong" is the right word for it.

The first thing you have to realize here is that you're dealing entirely in opinions—yours and your editor's. Now assuming that you've hired a professional (or more than one professional) who specializes in your genre or category–as you should!–whose opinion are you going to trust? Let's do a comparison.

Your Editor: Professional, highly skilled, trained, tons of experience, does this for a living, has the perspective of a reader who's never read the book before

You: Know the story/purpose inside and out, understand what everything means, understand what you're trying to impart, have all the missing pieces in your head

In case you don't see the issue, here it is: YOU are TOO CLOSE to your work. You can't see the issues clearly because you *simply can't see them*. How can you know if a description doesn't make sense when you know exactly what you're describing? How can you know if an explanation doesn't hit the mark when you know exactly what you're explaining? How can you know if a character isn't fully formed . . . You get the idea.

By the way, notice I didn't mention anything about *your* skill/experience level? That's because it doesn't matter . . .

When it comes to feedback from skilled, trained, experienced professionals, even the most experienced and successful authors bow to that expertise. And if they (and you!) are smart, they use these critiques to help them learn and grow and improve as authors. You may not realize it, but constructive criticism from editors (and beta readers, by the way) is one of the best educations you can get as an author. So take it that way and . . .

Manage Expectations

The best way to avoid a negative reaction to feedback is to get yourself ready for it. It's really easy to hope for a light edit with hardly any suggestions in it, but that's not the reality. More often than not, you're going to get a lot more redlining (inline suggestions) and comments than you expect, but if you expect a lot to begin with, you stand a much better chance of not being disappointed (or at least not as much as you could have been) or, on occasion, of being pleasantly surprised.

But what if you're really confident that the manuscript is in great shape? Doesn't matter. It's best to assume that you will have a lot of work to do once you get the manuscript back, even if you're confident that you've done a really good job. Again, this approach sets you up to feel relief and gratitude if the manuscript comes back pretty clean, and it helps mitigate your feeling disappointed, hurt, or angry if the manuscript comes in covered in red. You'll be much better prepared to tackle all those suggestions.

Don't Act on Your First Reaction

If you do have a negative emotional response to your feedback, don't act on it. You may find yourself rejecting very valid and important suggestions, denying your manuscript and your intended readers important improvements that they deserve. You may also deny yourself publishing opportunities by submitting a subpar manuscript when you could have submitted a much better one. And as noted in an article from Autocrit, "When you put all your energy into defending your work, you have no energy left to process the good advice you might have [been given]."

If you tend to be the confrontational type, you might also find yourself making accusations that can damage your relationship with your editor(s). And if you react publicly, like on social media or in an online review, you can really damage someone's professional reputation. You certainly don't want to answer their professional constructive criticism with reactionary destructive criticism, so for the good of everyone, including yourself, rein in those initial negative reactions, and here's how ...

Step Away and Come Back Later

This is one of the best strategies for dealing with those initial reactions. Just step away from the manuscript for a while—at least a day or two—and give yourself a chance to absorb the feedback and work through it. This is something that I've found effective for myself.

Perhaps ironically, as an editor, I find it very difficult to get critiqued. I don't know. I guess my brain is wired for giving it, not taking it. I often find myself getting a little defensive when getting feedback from my writing group. It's gotten better over the years because I recognize it in myself and have worked to calm it. Part of that process has been the realization that, more often than not, when

I go back to those comments days or weeks later, I agree with them! I may not agree with the specific suggestion, but I recognize that there's a problem, and I figure out how to fix it.

If I simply dismissed the suggestions that had me feeling defensive, I would never make the changes that ultimately lead me to much better writing. And all of that comes from the distance I create between receiving the suggestions and making the revisions, a distance that allows me to see those suggestions in a calmer, more objective light.

Take It One Criticism at a Time

So you've opened up your edited file and found page after page after page of red. Some pages have so many comments they don't all fit in the available space! You scroll and scroll and get more overwhelmed as you go. How are you ever supposed to get through all these suggestions!

Even if you agree with every single one of them, so many comments and suggestions can be truly over-whelming when you look at them as a whole, and the best way to deal with the volume of red you're facing is to focus in on one change at a time. Your feedback instantly becomes more manageable and less stressful regardless of the type of edit you're working through. Similarly . . .

Take Your Time

Don't rush through reviewing your editing feedback or making the suggested changes. Open up your schedule—reschedule any conflicting events or appointments that you can, send your family to a movie, spend a night or two at a hotel—and give yourself time to focus on the revision process. Rushing not only opens you up to a greater possibility of error, but it also causes the kind of stress and anxiety that we're working to avoid.

Don't Take It Personally

One of my favorite movie moments is in *You've Got Mail*. If you've seen it, you probably already know the scene I'm talking about. Tom Hanks is sitting in Meg Ryan's living room and telling her that his Barnes & Noble-inspired bookselling conglomerate running her little local bookshop out of business was "not personal." Her response, and I'm paraphrasing a bit here, is "What does that even mean? It's not personal. It was personal *to me*."

And that encapsulates the problem with people telling you that their constructive criticism isn't personal, because of course it's personal to you. So why do people like me keep saying that it's not personal? Because it's not personal *to your editor*. That's the point that we miss while we're licking our wounds. And if they've followed the requirements of constructive criticism correctly, they've focused on the writing, not the writer, ensuring that their feedback is entirely unpersonal.

Still, call it a punch to the gut or a stab to the heart, whether it's constructive or not, that criticism can really hurt. The way to protect yourself is to try to separate yourself from the manuscript. Here are a couple key points to consider:

1. **It's Not Your Baby.** Wait, what? Authors refer to their books as their babies all the time. It's a very popular metaphor, so what the heck am I talking about? You may think of your manuscript as being something you metaphorically birthed, but that's where the metaphor ends. Your manuscript doesn't care one bit about what you do to it—it's not a fragile thing that you have to care for and protect. It's OK for your manuscript to be extremely important to you, obviously, but try not to anthropomorphize it into your precious little darling. It's your art, not your child, as difficult as it may be to differentiate the two sometimes.

2. **It's Not About You.** One of the toughest ideas to internalize is that constructive criticism of your manuscript is not criticism of you as a person or even as a writer. It's not about you at all. It's about the words on the page and nothing more. Well, that's not quite true. It's about the words on the page and how well they will be able to connect with your readers. So it's about the words on the page and it's about the readers, but it's not about you. (Did I make that clear? It's not about you!)

Consider the Source

I've mentioned that I'm talking about constructive criticism from professionals, but you may choose to get feedback from others as well. Even if you don't, who are these professionals you've hired?

1. **Choose Professionals Wisely.** Take great care in selecting editors. Ensure they are a good match for you and your manuscript. They should specialize in your genre (sci-fi, romance, women's lit, etc.) or category (fiction, memoir, other nonfiction) as follows:

   - developmental editors: genre *and* category
   - line editors, copyeditors, proofreaders: category

   They should have plenty of demonstrable experience, and you should feel really good about hiring them. And if you've done your due diligence and have hired the right person/people, then you should trust them. There's no point in hiring someone you don't trust, so hire professionals you do trust so that you have the confidence of knowing that they know what they're talking about.

2. **Use Caution with Nonprofessionals.** It's not that you can't take nonprofessional opinions seriously. I take my writing group seriously, and none of them are professional editors. But I know that they have the best intentions in trying to help me improve, and I trust those intentions. But I would not have trusted my dad's opinion. I love my dear departed

father with all my heart, but he would have been a terrible person to ask for a writing critique, if only because he would have had no idea what he was doing. So consider who's giving you the feedback and whether or not that person is qualified to do so.

3. **Don't Read Reviews.** While you don't get reviews until *after* you're published and it's mostly too late at that point to do anything about it, this is still worth mentioning. First of all, your reviews aren't for you. They're for other readers. Second, they're rarely constructive (because they don't have to be). And third, they're often written by readers who don't know anything about writing. A five-star review can have you walking on clouds, but a bad review can ruin your whole week. Try not to read them.

Ask Questions

Just like authors can't always know when their writing is confusing, editors can't always know when their critiques are confusing. So if you have trouble understanding the what, how, or why of any comment or suggestion, ask for clarification. Especially when it comes to criticisms that upset you, it's good to chat it out in order to avoid misunderstanding. Oftentimes, discussing the criticism allows you to work through it and find a solution that you like, effectively turning a negative experience into a positive one and improving your manuscript in the process. And furthermore…

Ask What Inspired the Criticism

Sometimes you'll encounter criticisms for which you just can't figure out the why. You understand what the person wants you to do and how they want you to do it, but you just don't know *why* they want you to do it. And worse, you don't agree with the what or the how. How do you reconcile that?

You ask the person what's behind the suggested change so you can understand what inspired them to suggest it. According to story coach and editor Lisa Poisso, "You might find you agree about the underlying issue but come up with an entirely different way to fix it. But you can't do that if you dismiss a recommendation you don't like without understanding the reasoning that went into it."

For example, maybe your editor has recommended that you change a character's name to avoid confusion. Why would the name cause confusion? You like the character's name and you don't want to change it, and more importantly, you don't see how or why it would be confusing. The only person who's confused is you! So you ask the editor why they think the name is confusing. They explain that the character in question is named Anita and your main character is named Analisa, and the two names are so similar that readers might get the characters confused. Lightbulb!

So if you understand a suggestion but can't figure out why the person made it, ask. Even if you agree with the

change or just don't mind either way, you might learn
something if you ask why.

Remember that You Are in Charge

At the end of the day, it's your manuscript and the
changes you make or don't make are entirely up to you.
If you don't agree with a suggested change, don't make
it! You're in charge.

Now, having said that, remember that we're talking
about hiring professionals here, and presumably you
hired them for a reason. So don't just discount what
they've said out of hand. Give it some serious thought
first. In dealing with suggestions you don't agree with, I
recommend the following:

1. Go through the manuscript and accept/make all
   the changes you agree with. Consider the ones you
   don't agree with, but do nothing. Leave them as is.
2. Take a break from the manuscript, at least a day or
   two.
3. Go back with fresh eyes and consider the suggestions you didn't agree with. Do you still not agree
   with them? Do you need clarification for any of
   them? Go ahead and deal with the ones you're certain about and ask questions about the ones you
   aren't. Don't reject a suggestion until you're absolutely certain that you are not going to make the
   change.

When it comes to developmental changes, this process may look more like (1) *make a plan* for the changes you agree with, (2) take a break, then (3) go back over the changes you didn't agree with… Given the extent of revisions that some developmental changes require, you may have to decide what to do about the suggestions you don't like before you can start making any changes, even the ones you do like.

An author once apologized to me for not making all the changes I'd suggested in a copyedit, but accepting everything is neither expected nor required. You have to do what you believe to be best for your manuscript. Just be cautious in these decisions and ensure that you are, in fact, doing what's best for the *manuscript*, not what's best for *you* (no, they aren't the same thing). As long as you approach it in this way, then you can trust yourself to make the right decisions.

Say Thank You

OK, this one might seem a bit odd, but hear me out. First of all, this person has given you a lot of their time. Sure, you're paying for it, but still. They've done what you hired them to do, so a thank you is not out of the question. But more importantly, it's good for you to show gratitude for the criticism—good for you psychologically, I mean. It shows that you accept that they have given you a valid critique of your work, and even if you don't agree with all of it, that you appreciate the feedback.

This is a good kind-of Zen approach to receiving constructive criticism because gratitude can fill you up with yummy positiveness, whether you're giving it or receiving it. Gratitude is just a good thing to have in your life, and when you're able to show gratitude for a few hundred pages of criticisms, that's amazing! It's a genuine gift that you give to them and yourself. Yay!

Honorable Mentions

Here are some more tips for dealing with constructive criticism that didn't make the "favorites" list but are still good strategies to consider.

1. **Keep in mind the intent behind the criticism.** Which is what? To help you! Editors exist for the sole purpose of helping you improve your work. Try to keep that in mind at all times.

2. **Read to understand, not to respond.** This is a slight alteration to a piece of advice from the team at Asana who said, "*listen* to understand, not to respond." The point is the same however. When it comes to receiving constructive criticism, you must first and foremost try to understand it, then you can decide how to deal with it.

3. **Check your ego at the door.** Try to maintain some level of humility. You don't know everything (no one does), and you've hired a professional, after all. Set your ego aside, do yourself a favor, and listen to them.

4. **Consider that the greater the reaction, the truer the feedback.** I lifted this one from editor and contracts negotiator Janey Burton in her self-titled blog, but some clarification is needed. The idea here is that it's unlikely that you'll get angry over a suggestion that has no merit whatsoever. Of course, if *multiple* suggestions have no merit, you could be facing a bad edit, and that's certainly upsetting. Still, if a criticism really upsets you, there's a good chance it's a valid observation. At the very least, give it some serious thought. As Janey says, "Don't assume the [editor] is wrong. When they see things you didn't think were there, they're usually right."

5. **Look out for repeat criticism.** If you get repeat feedback from multiple reviewers, including your editor, take it to heart. If an issue is noticed by more than one person, it's an issue you need to deal with.

6. **Change your perspective.** Try to look at the criticism from a different angle and turn it from a negative to a positive. Instead of thinking of it as just criticism, think of it as an opportunity for improvement. As Leo Babauta says in his blog, *Zen Habits*, "without that constant improvement, we are just sitting still. Improvement is a good thing."

7. **Agree with the criticism.** When you find suggestions that you disagree with, especially if they upset you, try to flip the script and actually advocate for them. Can you convince yourself? You might

be surprised. And if it doesn't work, you'll have no doubt that it's not a change you're going to make.

8. **Don't be too critical of yourself.** Every manuscript ever written—*every one of them*—has had room for improvement at some point. First draft $\neq$ final draft. Ever. Think of your favorite author. Guess what. They have an editor! No one is perfect, and no one writes the perfect book, at least not without help (and, actually, not ever). So give yourself a break. Just because you received a lot of constructive criticism doesn't mean you aren't a good writer or that you can't become an even better one. Take a lesson from the NY Book Editors who said in their blog, "Don't let feedback shake your confidence in yourself. Look at all feedback as an opportunity for you to either dig your heels into what you believe or level up your skills."

Conclusion

Consider this quote from the career improvement site The Muse: "Feedback, even that which you don't agree with or didn't invite, is where growth, development, and breakthroughs happen."

Like it or not, editorial feedback is a non-negotiable part of the *serious* author journey. You might consider skipping editing, thinking that you know enough about writing to edit your own book, but have you heard the old adage "The doctor who treats [them/her/him]self has a fool for a patient"? Well, make the mental leap here: "The author who edits [them/her/him]self is not a serious author and doesn't care about learning or growing or improving or writing a great book and doesn't want to be successful."

OK, I might have gone a little overboard there, but I'm not actually wrong.

Unfortunately, if you want to learn and grow and succeed as an author, you absolutely must deal with feedback from editors and, if you so choose, from beta readers and other reviewers. *No one* is above it, and that includes the most successful authors out there—how do you think they got so successful?

But even constructive criticism can be tough to deal with, and learning about and implementing strategies like the ones in this book will help you to not only survive the criticism but use it to help improve your current manuscript and your writing in general. And remember, the more you learn about writing and the more you use what you've learned in your writing, the less editorial criticism you'll have to deal with it, which is the ultimate way to handle constructive criticism—remove the need for it!

(OK, you'll never remove the need for it entirely, but you can certainly minimize it, and that's pretty special. Good luck!)

NOTES

Bibliography

Babauta, Leo. "How to Accept Criticism with Grace and Appreciation." Zen Habits. Accessed March 29, 2025. https://zenhabits.net/how-to-accept-criticism-with-grace-and-appreciatio/.

Burton, Janey. "5 Ways to Deal with Honest Editorial Feedback." Janey Burton. July 22, 2024. https://janeyburton.com/5-ways-to-deal-with-editorial-feedback/.

Brodsky, Sam. "8 Therapist-Backed Tips for Taking Criticism Like a Champ." WonderMind. June 22, 2023. https://www.wondermind.com/article.

Ephron, Nora, dir. *You've Got Mail*. 1998. Warner Bros. Pictures.

"How to Deal Assertively with Criticism." Centre for Clinical Interventions. Accessed March 29, 2025. https://www.cci.health.wa.gov.au/-/media/CCI/Consumer-Modules/Assert-Yourself/Assert-Yourself---07----Dealing-With-Criticism-Assertively.pdf.

Lastoe, Stacey. "7 Tips That'll Help You Stop Taking Criticism So Personally (and Make it Easier to Move On)." The Muse. Updated August 4, 2022. https://www.themuse.com/advice/7-tips-thatll-help-you-stop-taking-criticism-so-personally-and-make-it-easier-to-move-on.

Martins, Julia. "How to Give (and Take) Constructive Criticism." Asana. August 16, 2024. https://asana.com/resources/constructive-criticism.

Poisso, Lisa. "How to Handle Editing and Feedback on Your Novel." Lisa Poisso. Accessed March 29, 2025. https://www.lisapoisso.com/2016/11/23/handle-editing-feedback/.

"The Writer's Game Plan for Dealing With Constructive Criticism." NY Book Editors. Accessed March 29, 2025. https://nybookeditors.com/2020/12/the-writers-game-plan-for-dealing-with-constructive-criticism/.

Welteroth, Elaine. "How to Handle Criticism: 7 Tips from MasterClass Instructors." MasterClass. May 19, 2022. https://shorturl.at/4nOT8.

"When Feedback Hurts: How to Handle Criticism as a Writer." Autocrit. Accessed March 29, 2025. https://www.autocrit.com/handle-criticism-writer/.